Ways to Enhance Your Self-Esteem

by Candy Semigran

A Workbook to Accompany

ONE-MINUTE SELF-ESTEEM: THE GIFT OF GIVING

Also by the Author

One-Minute Self-Esteem: The Gift of Giving

250 WAYS TO ENHANCE YOUR SELF-ESTEEM

2101 Wilshire Blvd., Santa Monica, CA 90403

Designed by Bruce A. Fox
Cover design by Mark Shoolery

Library of Congress Cataloging-in-Publication Data

Semigran, Candace
250 Ways to Enhance Your Self-Esteem

ISBN 0-940-73503-2

First Printing 1988
Printed in the United States of America

Dedication

This book is dedicated to you, the reader, and your commitment to more joy, peace, and love inside yourself. By doing so, and sharing it with the people around you, you are helping to create a world of greater harmony and understanding–a world in which we all can win.

Acknowledgements

SPECIAL THANKS:

- to everyone who has ever participated in an Insight Service Seminar for showing me the blessings in giving
- to the Insight Staff for sharing some of your favorite affirmations and exercises in giving
- to Bruce Fox for your design and for creatively adding examples and exercises from your experience at Insight Seminars
- to Sandy Barnert for your assistance in editing and organizing
- to Beth Hinman, Leigh Skinner-Fortson, and Olga Messina for your production assistance, and Mark Shoolery for your cover design
- to the Confederation of Underground Philanthropists for your inspiration and ideas about anonymous giving
- and to my two best friends–John-Roger and my husband, Stu–for your love, encouragement and support.

Introduction

Much as members of an orchestra "practice" to be the best they can be so that they can excel in concert and be proud, we as individuals can "practice" being the best we can be–and in that way increase our:

- Self-esteem
- Self-confidence
- Self-trust
- Peace of mind
- Self-love

This workbook is designed to be used along with my book *One-Minute Self-Esteem: The Gift of Giving*. If you haven't read *One-Minute Self-Esteem*, I suggest you read it first.

The exercises in this workbook are designed as practice sessions for you to enhance your own self-esteem. There are many ways to use this material. You could do one exercise a day, one a week or do them as often as you like. Play with these exercises! Have fun and enjoy yourself!

For most of the workbook, a pen or pencil will be the only supply you will need. For some exercises, you will find it useful to also have the following supplies available:

- Colored pens, pencils, crayons or markers
- Magazines, scissors and glue (if you want to do your Treasure Maps in the form of a collage)
- Extra blank paper
- A journal for writing

You may find that, as you use this workbook, it becomes a colorful scrapbook record of all the wonderful things about you–things to review and cherish as you grow in self-esteem.

Have fun and enjoy!

Candy Semigran

Gratitude

Make a list of the people and things in your life for which you are grateful.

For example, I am grateful for:

1. *My husband*
2. *My teacher*
3. *My friends*
4. *The ability to love*
5. *Beautiful sunsets*

I am grateful for:

1.

2.

3.

4.

5.

6.

7.

8.

9.

10.

(etc.)

Gratitude

This process can be done with a partner or you can do it by yourself using your journal. Answer the following questions. You may wish to go through the questions a number of times focusing on various people and things for which you are grateful:

For example,

1) *I am grateful for my wonderful relationship with my husband.*

2) *I receive so much joy, love, and fulfillment from giving, receiving, and sharing our lives together.*

3) *I could reach out to others more and give of myself and my loving and share more of myself with my friends.*

4) *I could acknowledge both my husband and myself more fully for how we give to our relationship.*

1) What are you grateful for?

2) Why are you grateful?

3) How could you create, promote or allow more of that into your life?

4) Who or what could you acknowledge more fully?

Positive Qualities

Make a list of at least 10 positive qualities about yourself.

For example, I am:

1. *Loving*
2. *Giving*
3. *Caring*
4. *Beautiful*
5. *Honest*

I am:

1.

2.

3.

4.

5.

6.

7.

8.

9.

10.

(etc.)

Forgiveness

Forgiveness of self and others is a very powerful process. Complete the following statements:

I forgive myself for:

1.

2.

3.

4.

5.

I forgive ________________________ for:
(fill in name)

1.

2.

3.

4.

5.

I forgive my mother for:

1.

2.

3.

4.

5.

I forgive ________________________ for:
(fill in name)

1.

2.

3.

4.

5.

I forgive my father for:

1.

2.

3.

4.

5.

I forgive ________________________ for:
(fill in name)

1.

2.

3.

4.

5.

Make a list of the blessings in your life.

For example,

1. *I have a wonderful loving husband.*
2. *I have terrific friends.*
3. *I love my work.*
4. *My life is full of loving, sharing and service.*
5. *My home is a very nurturing and peaceful environment.*

My blessings:

1.
2.
3.
4.
5.
6.
7.
8.
9.
10.

Appreciation

Taking time to appreciate yourself and others is a powerful tool to enhance your self-esteem.

For example, what I appreciate about myself is:

1. *My dedication*
2. *My courage*
3. *My self-discipline*
4. *My inner strength*
5. *My compassion*

What I appreciate about myself is:

1.
2.
3.
4.
5.

What I appreciate about my father is:

1.
2.
3.
4.
5.

What I appreciate about my mother is:

1.
2.
3.
4.
5.

What I appreciate about_______________is:
(fill in name)

1.
2.
3.
4.
5.

Appreciation

Write a letter to your parents. Tell them the things you appreciate about them. Tell them what you have learned from them. This exercise works even when your parents are no longer living or were absent during some part of your life. Let them know how much you care. If you want to mail it, you can. Otherwise it's just for you.

Dear Mom and Dad,

Love,

____

(your name)

Write a letter or short note to someone else in your life (grandparents, brother, sister, friends, teacher . . .) and let them know how much you appreciate them, the things you have learned from them and how much you care. Then mail it.

Today, spend at least five minutes in front of the mirror doing some positive self-talk as you look into your eyes.

Today, call or write or talk to someone you care about and tell them how grateful you are for their presence in your life.

Today, tell at least three people how beautiful or handsome they are.

Call someone you admire and look up to. Invite them to lunch and take time to talk and share with them about the qualities in them you admire.

Today, compliment at least three people on how attractive they look.

Today, tell at least three people how beautiful their eyes are.

Today, as you go through the day, tell yourself at least three positive compliments.

Appreciation

Choose someone you admire. Make a list of the things you admire about them.

I admire ________________________.
(fill in name)

The things I admire about ________________________ are:

1.
2.
3.
4.
5.
6.
7.
8.
9.
10.

________________________ is a mirror of me. The things I admire about ________________________ are also true of me.

How I manifest those qualities in my life is:

Self-Appreciation

Make a list of at least 50 positive qualities about yourself.

1.
2.
3.
4.
5.
6.
7.
8.
9.
10.
11.
12.
13.
14.
15.
16.
17.
18.
19.
20.
21.
22.
23.
24.
25.
26.
27.
28.
29.
30.
31.
32.
33.
34.
35.
36.
37.
38.
39.
40.
41.
42.
43.
44.
45.
46.
47.
48.
49.
50.

Write a letter to yourself and mail it.

Dear ________________________ ,

What I love best about you is . . .

Love,

____
(Signature)

Another way to do this exercise is to seal the letter in an envelope addressed to yourself, and then give it to a friend with a note attached reminding them to mail it in a few weeks or so.

Stand in front of a mirror and look in your eyes. Repeat to yourself out loud, "I LOVE YOU ________________________ (and fill in your name)." Don't be surprised if you feel uncomfortable or silly at first. I encourage you to do this every morning first thing after you get up, again during the day anytime you are in front of a mirror or walking by a building where you see your own reflection in the windows, and again at night before going to bed. This is one of those processes that takes only seconds to do and can make a big difference when done repeatedly. (It can take time to start believing these three words . . . especially if you have been hard on yourself in the past.)

Acknowledgement

Make a list of things you would like be acknowledged for by someone important in your life.

1.
2.
3.
4.
5.
6.
7.
8.
9.
10.

Now repeat them to yourself for at least 10 minutes, looking in a mirror or with your eyes closed.

Be a Friend to Yourself

This process will take about 15 minutes. Imagine you have one day to enhance a friend's self-esteem. How would you treat them? What kinds of things would you do and/or say to them? Write a list below:

1.

2.

3.

4.

5.

6.

7.

8.

9.

10.

Now go back and read over your list. How many of those things have you done for yourself in the last two weeks? Circle them on your list. Notice how many of the things you would do for a friend, you have done for yourself in the last two weeks. Is it more than half? Less than half? Acknowledge yourself for the things that you have done to be your own good friend.

Someone once said that if we treated our friends the way we treat ourselves, we wouldn't have any. I suggest that if you do more of those things on your list for yourself, you will enhance your own self-esteem.

Now choose something on your list that you want, can and will do for yourself this week and put a star next to it. You may want to choose a specific time to do this and mark it in your calendar. Remember to check it off once you have completed it.

Bragging

This process can be done by speaking out loud in front of a mirror, or by writing a list, or silently by sitting back with your eyes closed–whichever way you prefer. Take three minutes each day to brag about yourself to yourself. Review all of the great things you did today and how wonderful you are. These can be little things like helping someone across the street, complimenting someone at work, picking up trash in your neighborhood. You can brag about some of the good things you have done for yourself like doing your workout, eating healthy foods, and taking care of yourself, or some of the things you are grateful for like getting the job you wanted, having a wonderful relationship, getting a raise, and so forth.

The great things I did today are:

1.
2.
3.
4.
5.
6.
7.
8.
9.
10.

My Strengths

Make a list of the things that are your greatest strengths.

For example, my strengths are:

1. *My sensitivity*
2. *My determination*
3. *My compassion*
4. *My leadership*
5. *My loving*

My strengths are:

1.
2.
3.
4.
5.
6.
7.
8.
9.
10.

Friendship

Complete these statements:

A friend is someone who . . .

I am a great friend because I am . . .

Emptying the Garbage

Take 10 minutes to an hour each day and write about whatever is on your mind . . . your thoughts, feelings, problems. Without trying to think about something to write, write whatever is present with you. Don't worry about spelling or complete sentences or grammar–and don't re-read what you write. At the end of the time that you set aside for this process, tear up the paper without re-reading it. Then you can either throw it in the trash or if you have a fireplace, you can burn it. And then just start noticing how you feel. I like to think of this process as emptying out the garbage. Start by taking at least 10 minutes right now to do this on a separate sheet of paper.

EVERY DAY IN EVERY WAY I AM GETTING BETTER AND BETTER

Spend a few minutes each day (or as often as you'd like) repeating the above statement to yourself. You can write it or say it to yourself in a mirror. Say and write it at least 10 times at each sitting including right now.

1.

2.

3.

4.

5.

6.

7.

8.

9.

10.

Make a list of ways you can take better care of yourself.

For example, I can take better care of myself by:

1. Saying only positive things to myself.
2. Eating healthy foods.
3. Exercising regularly.
4. Relaxing on my days off.
5. Soaking in the hot tub tonight.
etc.

I can take better care of myself by:

1.

2.

3.

4.

5.

6.

7.

8.

9.

10.

Go do your favorite form of physical exercise. You might try something different (e.g., exercising in a really nice setting indoors or out of doors, wearing new exercise clothes that make you feel really good about yourself, or exercising with a good friend).

Get a haircut or manicure or pedicure. Be sure to let the person know just how you would like it and keep telling yourself how much you deserve it!

Ask someone for their assistance with a project you are doing. You don't have to "need" their help–it's okay just to want it.

Ask someone to play or dance with you.

Ask someone for a hug.

Ask someone for something you want that they might be able to give you or assist you in creating for yourself.

Buy yourself a new outfit, something that really makes you feel terrific! You might want to wear it out of the store so you can walk around and let people see how great you look.

Take an oil or bubble bath or jacuzzi. Make it very special by using candles or soft music or clean, soft towels hot out of the dryer. Be creative and have fun!

Eat dinner by candlelight with your favorite music playing softly in the background. Have a special meal–something you really enjoy.

Get a massage or have someone give you a long back rub. Be sure to ask to have it done just the way you like.

Take some time to read a favorite book. Set things up so you are really comfortable e.g., wear your most comfortable clothes or pajamas, fix a pot of tea or hot chocolate, etc.

Buy yourself something you have been wanting–as a gift from you to yourself. (You might want to have it gift wrapped at the store so you can open it when you get home!)

Take some quiet time to meditate or contemplate or do spiritual exercises–quiet time inside your own heart. Set up your environment the way you will be most comfortable for this.

Good News

Spend three to five minutes focusing on the good news about yourself. Make a list of the good news about yourself.

For example, the good news about me is:
1. *I am a very good student.*
2. *I'm a very enthusiastic person.*
3. *I'm a caring person.*
4. *I am a good cook.*
5. *I share my love, joy and happiness with others.*

The good news about me is:

1.

2.

3.

4.

5.

6.

7.

8.

9.

10.

Share the good news about yourself with:

a) A friend or family member, and
b) With yourself in front of a mirror.

Giving to Yourself

Buy yourself some flowers or a little toy–just because you are deserving of a gift.

I bought myself ________________________ today just because:

Affirming Worthiness

Write the following affirmation 10 times:

I am worthy of loving and being loved.

1.
2.
3.
4.
5.
6.
7.
8.
9.
10.

Repeat the affirmation to yourself in a mirror as you look into your eyes.

Affirming the Positive

Create your own positive affirmation according to these guidelines.

Start it with the words "I am . . . " and include action "-ing" words. It will be most effective if you keep it short and capture the essence of who you are. Make it positive, powerful, present-tense and passionate for yourself.

Then write it and say it to yourself at least 10 times.

For example,

I am a beautiful, elegant woman, trusting my heart,
giving and receiving love.
I am trusting my heart, radiating joy, and loving you and me.
I am a confident, sensitive, loving man; honestly accepting myself and freely
sharing my love with you.

My affirmation:

What's Beautiful About Me

Make a list entitled "What's beautiful about me is . . . ." Include things you like about your body, your personality, your intellect, your character–anything that comes to mind.

For example, what's beautiful about me is:

1. *I'm very loving*
2. *I'm a great friend*
3. *I'm honest*
4. *I have beautiful eyes*
5. *My sensitivity*

"What's Beautiful About Me Is . . . "

1.

2.

3.

4.

5.

6.

7.

8.

9.

10.

Hugging

You may have heard the saying: "Five hugs a day keep the doctor away." We don't know how much it really affects the doctor, however, we do know hugging can be very good for most people.

Do at least one of the following:

1. Hug a teddy bear.
2. Hug yourself.
3. Hug someone you love.
4. Ask for a hug from someone you care about.

Letting Go of Guilt and Self-Judgment

Answer the following series of questions and read the statement at the end out loud. Cycle through the questions, answering them several times before moving on to the next exercise.

For example,

1. *What do you judge about yourself?*
   I judge my body . . . that it's not a perfect "10".
2. *What do you tell yourself about that?*
   I tell myself that I'm not okay the way I am . . . that I am not beautiful . . . that I am not pretty . . . that I don't deserve to be beautiful and that I will never be a "10".
3. *What "should" you do?*
   I should stick to my diet and exercise program and lose weight and look beautiful.
4. *Is there anything you can do about that?*
   Yes. I can commit to myself and keep my agreements with myself. I can resume my diet and exercise program.
5. *How can you resolve the judgment inside yourself?*
   I can forgive myself. I can realize that I have done what I have done up until now and know that I've done the best I knew how at the time. I can acknowledge my beauty as I am. I can recognize that I can be my own worst enemy and I can forgive myself for judging myself.
6. *How can you be more loving?*
   I can love and accept myself the way I am. I can love the parts of my body that I have judged. I can start taking better care of myself and be gentler with myself.
7. *Will you do that?*
   Yes.

I accept myself and love myself. My loving is the most important part of my behavior.

1. What do you judge about yourself?

2. What do you tell yourself about that?

3. What "should" you do?

4. Is there anything you can do about that?

5. How can you resolve the judgment inside yourself?

6. How can you be more loving?

7. Will you do that?

I accept myself and love myself. My loving is the most important part of my behavior.

Letting Go of Resentment

Answer the following series of questions and read the statement at the end out loud. Cycle through the questions, answering them several times before moving on to the next exercise.

For example,

1. *What do you judge about others?*
   I judge others when they yell at people and treat them in an unloving way.
2. *What do you tell yourself about them?*
   I tell myself that people who yell at others are wrong, that they are unloving and unkind.
3. *What "should" they do?*
   They should be kind, loving, caring, and sensitive and demonstrate their caring in all of their communications.
4. *Is there anything you can do about that?*
   I can either accept their behavior and love them anyway or I can let them know that their behavior bothers me and I'd like to see them treat people better.
5. *How can you resolve the judgment inside yourself?*
   I can forgive them and realize they are probably doing the best they know how. I can realize that the standards of behavior that are right for me may not be right for others.
6. *How can you be more loving?*
   I can love them for who they are and communicate my loving to them regardless of how they communicate with me. I can also do what I can to assist them.
7. *Will you do that?*
   Yes.

I accept and love ________________________ (fill in their name). My loving for them is more important than their behavior.

1. What do you judge about others?

2. What do you tell yourself about them?

3. What "should" they do?

4. Is there anything you can do about that?

5. How can you resolve the judgment inside yourself?

6. How can you be more loving?

7. Will you do that?

I accept and love ________________________ (fill in their name). My loving for them is more important than their behavior.

Forgiveness

Take some quiet time to sit back with your eyes closed and review your day or week. If there is anything that you are judging yourself for, you can just say to yourself inwardly, "I forgive myself for ________________________ (and fill in the blank)."

If there is anything you've judged someone else for, you can just say to yourself inwardly, "I forgive ________________________ (fill in their name) for . . . (and complete the sentence)."

It's amazing how taking just a few minutes to complete and forgive, can make a big difference in the way you feel about yourself.

Self-Forgiveness

On a separate piece of paper write the following:

I want but can't ______________________ because I'm ______________________ .

Continue writing a paragraph or two about what you want that you can't have, do or be and the reasons you give yourself.

Next, write down these statements:

> I forgive myself for judging myself.
> I release and let go of all blocks I have placed in the way of my having, doing or being who and what I want.
> I am loving myself and I am worthy.

Beneath that, sign your name.

Now tear it up and throw it away.

On a separate piece of paper write the following:

I'll never ______________________ because I'm ______________________ .

Continue writing a paragraph or two about what you want that you can't have, do or be and the reasons you give yourself.

Next, write down these statements:

> I forgive myself for judging myself.
> I release and let go of all blocks I have placed in the way of my having, doing or being who and what I want.
> I am loving myself and I am worthy.

Beneath that, sign your name.

Now tear it up and throw it away.

Self-Forgiveness

On a separate piece of paper write the following:

I'm not good enough to ____________________ because I'm ____________________ .

Continue writing a paragraph or two about what you want that you can't have, do or be and the reasons you give yourself.

Next, write down these statements:

> I forgive myself for judging myself.
> I release and let go of anything I have ever held against myself.
> I am loving myself and I am worthy.

Beneath that, sign your name.

Now tear it up and throw it away.

On a separate piece of paper write the following:

I'm afraid of ______________________ .

Continue writing a paragraph or two about the things in yourself you judge or disaprove of and the reasons you give yourself.

Next, write down these statements:

> I am relaxed and trusting in the perfect plan that is unfolding for me.
> I always do the best I can with what I know and use everything for my advancement.
> I am loving myself and I am worthy.

Beneath that, sign your name.

Now tear it up and throw it away.

Self-Forgiveness

On a separate piece of paper write the following:

I'm the hardest on myself about __________________________ .

Continue writing a paragraph or two about the things in yourself you judge or disaprove of and the reasons you give yourself.

Next, write down these statements:

> I forgive myself for judging myself.
> I give myself total unconditional acceptance as a loving and worthy individual.
> I always do the best I can with what I know and use everything for my advancement.

Beneath that, sign your name.

Now tear it up and throw it away.

On a separate piece of paper write the following:

I am too __________________________ .

Continue writing a paragraph or two about the things in yourself you judge or disaprove of and the reasons you give yourself.

Next, write down these statements:

> I forgive myself for judging myself.
> I give myself total unconditional acceptance as a loving and worthy individual.
> I always do the best I can with what I know and use everything for my advancement.

Beneath that, sign your name.

Now tear it up and throw it away.

Positive Self-Talk

Write or repeat the following statements to yourself as many times and as often as you'd like:

I accept and love myself. My loving is the most important part of my behavior.

I accept and love ________________________ (fill in the blank with a friend's name). My loving for them is more important than their behavior.

(Remember that when you accept or love or forgive someone, you are the one who receives the most benefit.)

Write and repeat to yourself at least 10 times the following statement:

I am worthy for who I am, not for what I do. I am enough.

1.
2.
3.
4.
5.
6.
7.
8.
9.
10.

Loving Your Self

Listen to the tape from this package entitled "Meditation for Loving Yourself." Then, if you want to, spend some time writing about or drawing a picture of how you feel.

Complete the following questions:

For example,

1. *What does taking care of yourself mean to you?*
   Spending time with friends
2. *What do you want?*
   A vacation in Hawaii
3. *What experience are you looking for?*
   Freedom, relaxation, peace
4. *How could you get it?*
   Spending some quiet time at home. Instead of waiting for my vacation, I could play some relaxing music and read a favorite book.

1. What does taking care of yourself mean to you?

2. What do you want?

3. What experience are you looking for?

4. How could you get it?

Compliments

Give at least three people compliments today. Write down their names and the compliment below.

1.

2.

3.

Give yourself a compliment as you look at yourself in the mirror (write it down, too). Also notice what about the compliments you gave others today is also true about you.

Heart-Talk

Have a "heart-talk"with your family and friends.

The purpose of this heart-talk is to give each person an opportunity to talk honestly, respectfully, and caringly to each member of the group, and to let his or her words be heard. It can be done in families or groups of all sizes and varieties.

This process takes about five to ten minutes per person. Start by asking everyone to sit down together in a circle. Ask who wants to go first and have them sit in a chair which will be the designated "heart seat." The only job of the person in this seat is to listen and to receive as, one at a time, the group members take turns giving feedback by completing the first sentence. After each member has taken a turn, go around the circle again and complete the second sentence, then the third, etc., until all the sentences have been completed by every member.

Then it is another member's turn to sit in the heart seat and receive the loving and caring communication. Repeat this process until everyone has had their turn.

Sentences to complete:

1. What I like or appreciate about you is . . .
2. What I would like more of from you is . . .
3. One thing that I could give more of to you is . . .
4. One thing I think is special about our family (or group) is . . .
5. One thing that I want to thank you for is . . .

Feel free to add to or adapt these statements to fit the situation. For instance, if you do this in a situation where people aren't as familiar, you could say things like:
What I respect about you is . . .
How I think you are doing a good job is . . .
The way I think I could be more helpful to you is . . .
What I always notice about you that I like is . . .
Just choose wording that your group will feel comfortable with.

Here are some suggestions:
When you are in the heart seat, just listen without answering back or making comments.
Make eye contact as you both deliver and receive your communications.
Practice blending honesty and loving in your communications.

Have fun and allow the specialness of your group to continue to flourish!

Heart-Talk

Have a heart-talk with a close friend or family member. During the heart-talk, complete the following statements:

1. What I appreciate about you is . . .
2. What I would like more of in our relationship is . .
3. What I would like less of in our relationship is . . .
4. The way I could give more in our relationship is . . .

This process is great to do with a partner, your spouse, your child, as a family, or with a friend. Decide who is going to go first. That person will be Partner A. Partner A then asks Partner B for something that Partner B can give them within the next five minutes (e.g., a back rub, a foot massage, a shoulder massage, a song, a poem, a dance, a joke, a hug) something nurturing that Partner B could give them.

If Partner B doesn't want to give Partner A what Partner A asks for, Partner A asks for something else. Partner B's job is to be honest. Partner A's job is to keep asking until they get a YES. Then take five minutes for Partner B to give to Partner A what they asked for. After five minutes, switch and it is Partner B's turn to do the asking, and Partner A's to do the giving.

Invite a friend to breakfast, lunch or dinner. Your treat. No special occasion, just an opportunity to be together and share. Afterward, write about your experience and what you learned about your relationship with your friend and with yourself.

Spend time with a friend or family member asking for and giving and receiving acknowledgment for things you have completed. Have fun with this. Let the acknowledgment in. You can also ask for a standing ovation!

Spend an evening with someone you love–in total silence–giving to each other without talking. This could include any silent giving or sharing experience such as holding hands, looking into each other's eyes, going for a walk, giving each other back rubs, etc.

Send a card to someone you love and let them know how much you care.

Write about how you felt doing this. You can also write about how you think the person who received your message of loving might feel.

Asking

Sometimes we don't get what we want because we are afraid to ask. Answer the following questions:

For example,

1. *What do you want that you don't ask for?*
   "A computer for our home."
2. *Whom don't you ask? Be specific.*
   "My husband."
3. *What is the fear?*
   "He'll think it costs too much and that I always spend too much money, and he'll say no."
4. *What is the worst that could happen?*
   "He'll say no, get mad at me, and say he wants a divorce because I'm always spending too much."
5. *What is the best that could happen?*
   "He'll say yes, we'll get the computer, and I'll write the book I've been talking about."
6. *What's likely to happen?*
   "He'll want to investigate prices and sit down and discuss it–and then he'll say yes."
7. *Will you ask for it?*
   "Yes."
8. *When?*
   "Tonight."

1. What do you want that you don't ask for?

2. Whom don't you ask? Be specific.

3. What is the fear?

4. What is the worst that could happen?

5. What is the best that could happen?

6. What is likely to happen?

7. Will you ask for it?

8. When? (Write it in your appointment book or calendar.)

What Can I Give?

Ask yourself, what is there that you could give to people that would have the value of love, compassion, joy, justice, mercy, and truth? What is it that you could give that can make a difference in someone's life? As well as your own? How about your heart? What would it be like if you were giving of your loving heart?

Cycle through the first three questions repeatedly. When you seem to reach your bottom line for question #3 and start coming up with the same answer, go on to question #4 and then start over. If you do this with a friend, take about five to ten minutes each so both of you have the opportunity to answer the questions.

1) What can you give?
2) How can you give that?
3) What experience are you looking for?

---

4) What can you give?

Anonymous Giving

Write and send a poem or card to someone. Make sure you don't let them know it's from you.

Give some flowers to someone you care about, but don't let them know who the flowers are from. Then write about how you feel or draw a picture to express your feelings.

Buy a gift–something you have been wanting for yourself–and give it away. Yes, give what you've been wanting to someone else and do it anonymously. How do you feel?

What joy do you think your gift might bring them?

Buy a little toy for a child and hide it in their room. Then see if you can be around when they find it and observe their process. What was their reaction? What experience did they seem to be having?

How do you feel about being a giver?

Leave some change in a phone booth for the next person to find.

Leave your waiter or waitress a thank-you card in addition to a tip.

Fill up a parking meter, even when you are on foot.

Go up to a person on the street, hand them a dollar and say, "I think you dropped this," and walk away quickly.

Pick up trash that is lying around your neighborhood.

Say nice things about someone you dislike.

Pay for the car(s) behind you in a toll booth. Then drive on.

Have flowers sent to someone at work who works very hard but doesn't get much acknowledgment.

At a market, give the checker $25 or $50 and tell them it's to be applied anonymously to the next person's bill.

Drop some change in a public place and leave it for someone else to find.

Send a thank-you card to a public servant.

Leave a thank-you card on the windshield of a police officer's car.

Leave small cloth bags filled with pennies in a schoolyard just before recess.

Pay for a stranger's meal in a restaurant–without letting them know you did it.

Pay a bill anonymously for a friend who might be having a hard time.

Once a month send a holiday card or gift to a friend, anonymously.

Ask your dentist, doctor, lawyer or veterinarian if you may pay the bill for a client who might have trouble otherwise.

Buy two theater tickets and give them to someone anonymously.

Practice making a contribution of money or clothing to a non-profit organization without requiring a receipt for tax purposes.

Get a small group of friends together and do a job for a friend. While one of you gets the recipient of your good deeds out of the house for a movie or something, the rest of the group can paint their kitchen or do something else that needs doing.

Contact a local minister or service group and do a service project for a perfect stranger.

Become a "guardian angel" for a friend, periodically throughout the year giving gifts, cards, etc. anonymously.

Send a present to one of society's servants who aren't often acknowledged–an IRS agent, a dentist, a politician, a teacher.

Go out of your way to greet a former enemy with kindness. Don't explain why you are doing this; just be nice to them.

Clean out your closet and house and give away items of clothing, toys, etc. that you no longer need. Give them to the charity of your choice.

As you go through your closet and house, give away an item of clothing, a toy, etc. that you really like and still use. Give it to the charity of your choice.

Drop some money into the shopping bag of a stranger at a grocery store–don't let them see you do it.

Prepare a meal for someone in need and have someone else take it to them–from an anonymous friend.

Arrange for a special treat to be delivered to someone you work with–to reward their good work–and do it anonymously.

Send an anonymous gift to someone in a hospital or convalescent home.

Visit a shut-in and take them out for a picnic lunch or for a walk or shopping, etc.

Make a list of at least three ways you could be of service to your family this week. Then do them.

Visit a convalescent or children's hospital. Take flowers to a patient there. Prepare a few sack lunches and give them to the homeless. Contact a local church and find out someone who needs assistance in your community (e.g., a house cleaned, a meal prepared, a room painted, etc.). Choose some way that you can be of service in your community.

Together with some friends, do a service project in your community (e.g., cleaning up a park, a beach or public place, paint or fix up the home of someone who is in need, etc.).

Select a local organization, your church group, school, educational organization, hospital, convalescent home, or service organization and volunteer time on a regular basis (i.e., once a week or more) where you just give and do whatever is needed and your service is your reward.

With a friend or family member, make one to twenty sack lunches. Take them to a local park or community area and give them to people who are hungry.

Handling Incompletions

Make a list of the projects you have at work that are incomplete. Go through the list and mark each item in one of three ways. Projects that you intend to complete, you can do right now if they take less than five minutes. Otherwise set a completion date or schedule a time to do them in your calendar or appointment book. You may decide that you really aren't going to ever do some things so you can declare them done and cross them off the list. There may be some items you can delegate to someone else. You can mark them with the person's name. Refer back to this list and cross things off as you or the person you have delegated to, complete them.

To do:	Complete by:	Delegated to:	Completed on:
1.			
2.			
3.			
4.			
5.			
6.			
7.			
8.			
9.			
10.			

Handling Incompletions

Make a list of the projects you have at home that are incomplete. Go through the list and mark each item in one of three ways. Projects that you intend to complete you can do right now if they take less than five minutes. Otherwise set a completion date or schedule a time to do them in your calendar or appointment book.

You may decide that you really aren't going to ever do some things, so you can declare them done and cross them off the list. There may be some items you can delegate to someone else. You can mark them with the person's name. Refer back to this list and cross things off as you, or the person you have delegated to, complete them.

To do:	Declared Complete:	Delegated to:	Completed on:
1.			
2.			
3.			
4.			
5.			
6.			
7.			
8.			
9.			
10.			

Clean out your garage or storage area. Give away anything you haven't used in at least a year and don't plan to use in the future.

Clean out all of your kitchen cabinets. As a reward, buy yourself a small gift for the kitchen–it could be a neat utensil or gadget, a picture or saying or a bright new dish towel.

Clean out your refrigerator. When you are finished you might want to put up an affirmation or a treasure map on the door where you can see it.

Clean out your closet and drawers–give away anything you haven't worn in over a year to someone else who might be able to use it. You can also try arranging your clothes in a different way and when you get dressed try new combinations of clothing and accessories.

Handling Incompletions

Make a list of books you have begun and never finished. Cross off the names of any books that, upon considering, you realize you honestly do not intend to read. Put a star next to the titles of the books you most want to read (this could be because you have been looking forward to reading them, or you need to for work or school, etc.). Schedule a time in the next week when you will continue reading one of them.

1.

2.

3.

4.

5.

6.

7.

8.

9.

10.

Handling Incompletions

Make a list of any equipment you own or use that is broken and needs repair and schedule a time to take care of it in the next week or two.

1.
2.
3.
4.
5.
6.
7.
8.
9.
10.

Make a list of letters you need to write. Write one now. Plan to handle the rest in a timely way. This could include setting a goal of writing at least one letter per week, or scheduling one day when you will regularly handle correspondence.

1.
2.
3.
4.
5.
6.
7.
8.
9.
10.

Handling Incompletions

Make a list of phone calls you haven't returned or need to make. If possible, make at least one of them right now. If not, schedule a time in your calendar or appointment book to do so.

1.

2.

3.

4.

5.

6.

7.

8.

9.

10.

Make a list of gardening projects you have that are incomplete. If possible, do at least one of them right now. If not, schedule a time in your calendar or appointment book to do so.

1.

2.

3.

4.

5.

6.

7.

8.

9.

10.

Handling Incompletions

Make a list of financial projects you have that are incomplete. Go through the list and mark each item in one of three ways. Projects that you intend to complete you can do right now if they take less than five minutes. Otherwise set a completion date or schedule a time to do them in your calendar or appointment book.

You may decide that you really aren't going to ever do some things, so you can declare them done and cross them off the list. There may be some items you can delegate to someone else. You can mark them with the person's name. Refer back to this list and cross things off as you, or the person you have delegated to, complete them.

To do:	Declared Complete:	Delegated to:	Completed on:
1.			
2.			
3.			
4.			
5.			
6.			
7.			
8.			
9.			
10.			

Loving

Ask a family member or close friend to tell you how much they love you.

Write about what they said and about how you feel.

Make a list of everything in your life that is not totally the way you want it. Beside each item list your next action step.

For example,

1. My teeth	*1. Make dental appointment*
2. My weight	*2. Call the diet center*
3. My shoes	*3. Take shoes to repair shop*
4. My clothes	*4. Mend skirt*
5. The VCR	*5. Take VCR to repair shop*

Write your next steps in your planning calendar (i.e., schedule them to be handled). One at a time handle them, then check them off on your list.

Item	**Next Step**
1.	1.
2.	2.
3.	3.
4.	4.
5.	5.
6.	6.
7.	7.
8.	8.
9.	9.
10.	10.

Demonstrating Your Loving

My loving is the most important part of my behavior.

The ways I could demonstrate my loving more to myself and others are:

1.

2.

3.

4.

5.

6.

7.

8.

9.

10.

Strengths

Ask a family member or close friend to tell you what they think your strengths are. Make a list of them:

1.
2.
3.
4.
5.
6.
7.
8.
9.
10.

Think of one of your best friends. Make a list of what you like, admire and respect about them:

1.

2.

3.

4.

5.

Spend some time with them and share these feelings from your heart. Then ask them to share with you what they like, admire and respect about you. (This can be done very simply and conversationally if they are not used to sharing feelings so openly.) Notice how much you have in common and how you serve as mirrors for each other.

Ideal Scenes

If I could do anything I wanted to, I would . . .

If I could have anything I wanted to, I would . . .

If I could be any way I wanted to be I would . . .

Stand in front of a full-length mirror dressed in one of your favorite outfits. Observe your image in the mirror–look at how you stand, ask yourself how you feel, listen to what kinds of things you are saying to yourself inwardly as you do this. Write about how you feel:

Stand in front of a full-length mirror dressed in one of your favorite outfits. Draw a picture of yourself as you see yourself in the mirror.

Stand in front of a full-length mirror dressed in one of your favorite outfits. Write down what you like about this person and what you see.

Stand in front of a full-length mirror dressed in one of your favorite outfits. Write down what you see that you don't like or would like to have differently. How would you change those things? (Be careful how you talk to yourself in this exercise–be very gentle and supportive.)

Stand naked in front of a full-length mirror. Observe your image in the mirror–look at how you stand, ask yourself how you feel, listen to what kinds of things you are saying to yourself inwardly as you do this. Write about how you feel:

Stand naked in front of a full-length mirror. Draw a picture of yourself as you see yourself in the mirror.

Stand naked in front of a full-length mirror. Write down what you like about this person and what you see.

Stand naked in front of a full-length mirror. Write down what you see that you don't like or would like to have differently. How would you change those things? (Be careful how you talk to yourself in this exercise–be very gentle and supportive.)

Write a poem or love song dedicated to loving the parts of you that you have judged. Appreciate those parts of yourself.

Draw a picture of how you would like to look. Be sure the picture shows how good you feel about yourself and how happy you are!

Write a paragraph or do a mind map about your ideal scene regarding how you would like to look.

For example,

MY HEALTHY BODY

- NUTRITION
  - EAT MORE HEALTHY FOODS
  - NO SUGAR ON BREAKS
- EXERCISE
  - GYM 3X WEEK
  - WALK AT LUNCH
  - BUY EXERCISE OUTFIT
- POSITIVE IMAGE
  - MIRROR WORK
  - AFFIRMATIONS
  - COMPLIMENT MYSELF
  - BUY NEW CLOTHES
- APPEARANCE
  - TEETH
    - SMILE OFTEN
    - FLOSS DAILY
    - CHECK-UP
  - SKIN
    - SCRUB NIGHTLY
    - HAVE A FACIAL
  - HAIR
    - BUY CONDITIONER
    - NEW STYLE
  - NAILS
    - GET MANICURE
    - COLOR POLISH
    - BUY

Write down your goals for the next six months for your body, health and appearance.

For example,

1. *Lose 20 pounds*
2. *Exercise for a minimum of 20 minutes, three times per week.*
3. *Buy four new outfits (or spend $1000 on clothes.)*
4. *Eat healthful meals.*
5. *Get plenty of rest.*

My goals for my body, health and appearance in the next six months:

1.

2.

3.

4.

5.

6.

7.

8.

9.

10.

etc.

Make a Treasure Map for your body, health and appearance–how you will look when you reach your goals. A Treasure Map can be a drawing, painting, or collage depicting how you will look, feel, or act when you have reached your goal. The best Treasure Maps produce enthusiasm and encouragement for achieving your goals.

Examples of positive affirmations that you can repeat regarding your body, health, and appearance:

I am enjoying my slim, fit, beautiful body at its perfect weight.

I am trim, muscular, and well-defined standing tall in my healthy body.

I love the energy and radiant health I experience with my lean, well-toned and flexible body at its perfect weight.

I am creating a trimmer, healthy, beautiful body.

I am relaxed, accepting my beauty and growing healthier every day.

What I am grateful for about my body is:

1.

2.

3.

4.

5.

6.

7.

8.

9.

10.

etc.

Make a list of personal affirmations for your body, health, and appearance.

For example,

I look sensational and feel terrific wearing my 31" waist Calvin Klein Jeans.
I love the healthy way my mouth feels flossing every day.
I am joyfully anticipating exercising three times this week because when I do, my body feels so good.

My positive affirmations for my body, health and appearance:

1.

2.

3.

4.

5.

Now spend ten minutes repeating these in front of the mirror. Remember to smile!

Take a few minutes to close your eyes and visualize yourself having already reached your goals regarding your body, health, and appearance. How do you look? How do you feel? What positive self-talk is going on? Hear your friends complimenting you.

Relationships

Write a paragraph or create a mind map of your ideal scene regarding your friends, relationships and family. Include all the details of how you would like all of your relationships to be.

For example,

I am sharing wonderful times with my loving friends. There is a tremendous level of support and encouragement amongst us all. It is easy for me to make new friends and I enjoy meeting people wherever I go. I am enjoying a fulfilling, exciting relationship with my loving husband. We are constantly growing and learning together with great respect and understanding. I have a close relationship with my family. We enjoy each other's company whenever we are together and grow closer with time.

Relationships

My goals in the area of my relationships with my family and friends for the next six months are:

1.

2.

3.

4.

5.

6.

7.

8.

9.

10.

etc.

Relationships

Make a Treasure Map showing your wonderful, fulfilling relationships. Include pictures of yourself, and your family and friends doing the things you have written down as your goals. Cut out phrases from magazines or write your own that describe the experiences you want to have.

Examples of positive affirmations that you can repeat in the area of relationships:

It is easy for me to relate with my boss, my peers and my subordinates in ways that are uplifting and productive for all concerned.

I am bringing joy and love to all my relationships.

I am confidently and compassionately interacting with everyone I meet.

I am trusting myself and communicating honestly.

I am finding simple solutions for win/win results in my relationships.

My loving for people is more important than their behavior.

My heart is a love magnet attracting beautiful, caring people into my life.

What I am grateful for regarding my relationships, my family and friends is:

1.

2.

3.

4.

5.

6.

7.

8.

9.

10.

etc.

Relationships

Make a list of personal affirmations for your relationships.

For example,

I am having fun and making new friends.
I am bringing joy and love to all my relationships.

My positive affirmations about my relationships:

1.
2.
3.
4.
5.

Now spend ten minutes repeating these with joy and enthusiasm.

Close your eyes for a few minutes and visualize yourself having already reached your goals for your relationships. How do you look? How do you feel? Hear yourself talking with your friends and family members. Write about your experience:

Write a paragraph or create a mind map of your ideal scene regarding your relationship with yourself.

For example,

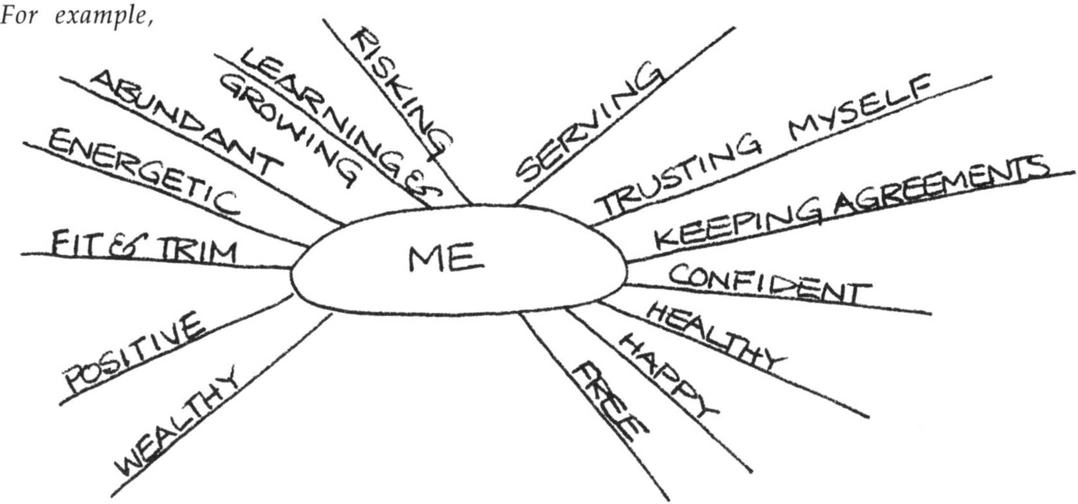

My goals in the area of my relationship with myself for the next six months are:

1.

2.

3.

4.

5.

6.

7.

8.

9.

10.

etc.

Make a Treasure Map showing the completion of your goals for your relationship with yourself. Show how much you enjoy being with you.

Examples of positive affirmations that you can repeat regarding your relationship with yourself:

I am enjoying relaxed freedom and heightened energy, tracking and completing my inner and outer agreements.

I am using only positive self-talk to increase my self-esteem and support my personal goals.

I am maintaining a healthy, enjoyable balance in my personal and professional lifestyles.

In challenging situations I remain relaxed and focused on positive outcomes.

I love myself just the way I am. I know that I am enough.

What I am grateful for regarding my relationship with myself is:

1.
2.
3.
4.
5.
6.
7.
8.
9.
10.

etc.

Make a list of personal affirmations for your relationship with yourself.

For example,

I love myself just the way I am.
The time I spend with myself is a time for joy and nurturing.
I am my own best friend.

My positive affirmations about my relationship with myself:

1.

2.

3.

4.

5.

Now spend ten minutes repeating them. Focus on being glad to spend time with yourself.

Close your eyes for a few minutes and visualize yourself having already reached your goals for your relationship with yourself. How do you look? Hear yourself saying positive things about yourself. How do you feel being your own best friend? Write about what that was like:

Write a paragraph or create a mind map of your ideal scene regarding your education, job or career.

For example,

Education/Job/Career

My goals in the area of my education, job or career for the next six months are:

1.

2.

3.

4.

5.

6.

7.

8.

9.

10.

etc.

Examples of positive affirmations you can repeat regarding education, job, or career:

I bring success, abundance, and upliftment to all involved in my professional interactions.

I am a brilliantly fast reader, comprehending and retaining all that is and will be useful to me.

I am confidently interacting with people as I am serving those who come to me.

I daily increase the value I create for myself, my family, and my organization.

I have perfect work in a perfect way, giving perfect service for perfect pay.

Make a Treasure Map showing the completion of your goals for your education, job or career. You might want to include pictures of yourself doing the job, or in front of the school, in a cap and gown holding a diploma, or in business attire behind a big desk. You could paste in, print or type your name with your degree or job title, or include a school emblem or company logo. Be creative and have fun!

Education/Job/Career

Make a list of personal affirmations for your education, job or career.

For example,

I am completing my bachelor's degree in accounting by June, 1990.
I love my new job as a travel agent.
I am a successful marketing consultant and my services are in great demand.

My positive affirmations about my education/job/career:

1.

2.

3.

4.

5.

Now spend ten minutes repeating your affirmations. As you do this, know that all you have to do to move ahead is take the next action steps.

Close your eyes for a few minutes and visualize yourself having already reached your goals for your education, job or career. How do you look? How do you feel? Hear yourself talking about your advancement and accomplishments. Write about how you feel:

Education/Job/Career

What I am grateful for regarding my education, job and career is:

1.

2.

3.

4.

5.

6.

7.

8.

9.

10.

etc.

Finances/Abundance/Prosperity

Write a paragraph or create a mind map of your ideal scene regarding the areas of personal finances, abundance and prosperity in your life.

For example,

> *My ideal scene includes owning my own home, having a positive cash flow, paying off all of my debts, having a growing and healthy financial reserve, and having the ability to travel and give gifts to those I love and care about; always having more than I need.*

Finances/Abundance/Prosperity

My goals in the areas of personal finance, abundance and prosperity for the next six months are:

1.
2.
3.
4.
5.
6.
7.
8.
9.
10.

etc.

Examples of positive affirmations that you can repeat regarding finances, abundance, and prosperity:

I am comfortably receiving all of the money and resources I need to do my highest level of work on this planet.

Large sums of money come to me quickly for the highest good of all concerned.

I love the feeling of freedom I have with a positive cash flow and a growing, healthy reserve.

I bring success, abundance, and upliftment to everyone involved in my personal and professional interactions.

I deserve to be abundantly wealthy and successful.

Make a Treasure Map showing the completion of your goals for personal finance, abundance and prosperity. You can really have fun finding pictures of things you would like to have and the way you would like to live. Cut out or write words and phrases that support your attitude of abundance. Be sure to put a picture of yourself somewhere in the Treasure Map, whether it is driving a new car or doing something you have always wanted to do.

Finances/Abundance/Prosperity

Make a list of personal affirmations for your personal finances, abundance and prosperity.

For example,

I feel safe and secure knowing I am abundant in all things for the highest good.
I am balancing my checkbook every month and managing my finances with ease and accuracy.
I am easily and joyfully creating abundance by doubling my income this year.

My positive affirmations about my personal finances, abundance and prosperity:

1.

2.

3.

4.

5.

Now spend ten minutes repeating your affirmations. As you do this, keep focusing on how much you deserve to have all these things.

Close your eyes for a few minutes and imagine having already reached your goals for your personal finances, abundance and prosperity. How do you look? How do you feel? Hear yourself talking about how abundant you are.

Finances/Abundance/Prosperity

What I am grateful for regarding my personal finances, abundance and prosperity is:

1.

2.

3.

4.

5.

6.

7.

8.

9.

10.

etc.

Write a paragraph or create a mind map of your ideal scene regarding recreation, travel or hobbies in your life.

For example,

My husband and I are enjoying riding our bicycles, jogging and doing our aerobic workouts. We are enjoying taking trips with friends and traveling throughout Germany, the Soviet Union, and Europe.

Recreation/Travel/Hobbies

My goals in the areas of my recreation, travel or hobbies for the next six months are:

1.

2.

3.

4.

5.

6.

7.

8.

9.

10.

etc.

Examples of positive affirmations that you can repeat regarding recreation, travel, and hobbies:

We are joyfully creating all of the resources we need to travel to Europe with our friends this summer.

I am confident and comfortable singing before large audiences.

I am enjoying the free time I have to be with, share, and play with my children.

I am having lots of fun learning to cross-country ski.

I feel so peaceful and relaxed, listening to my favorite music.

Make a Treasure Map showing the completion of your goals for recreation, travel or hobbies. Show yourself having fun doing things you have always dreamed of doing or going to far away places. You may even want to include pictures of friends doing those things with you.

Make a list of personal affirmations for your recreation, travel or hobbies.

For example,

I am having a wonderful time, relaxing on the beach in Maui.
I am so excited about receiving my pilot's license by September 30th.
My tennis game is improving every time I play.

My positive affirmations about my recreation, travel or hobbies:

1.

2.

3.

4.

5.

Now spend ten minutes repeating them. As you do, keep focusing on all the exciting details of your plans.

Close your eyes for a few minutes and visualize yourself having already reached your goals for your recreation, travel or hobbies. How do you look? How do you feel? Hear yourself talking about how much fun you had. Write about your experience:

Recreation/Travel/Hobbies

What I am grateful for regarding my recreation, travel or hobbies is:

1.
2.
3.
4.
5.
6.
7.
8.
9.
10.

etc.

Home

Write a paragraph or create a mind map of your ideal scene regarding your home. (If you want to move into a new home, use this process to create your ideal scene for the home you want.)

For example,

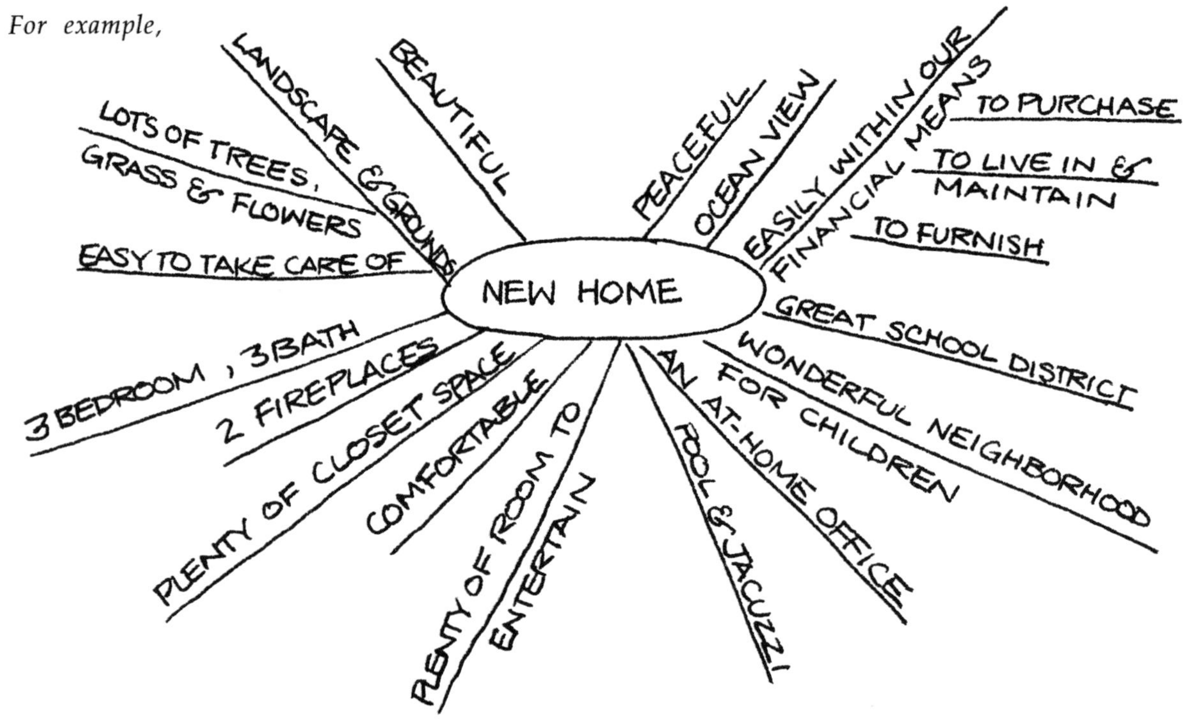

Home

My goals regarding my home for the next six months are:

1.

2.

3.

4.

5.

6.

7.

8.

9.

10.

etc.

Examples of positive affirmations you can repeat regarding your home:

I am creating a home of peace, joy, love, and beauty for myself and my family.

My home is a sanctuary surrounded by beautiful green trees and colorful fragrant flowers.

I am relaxing, creating harmony and balance as I enjoy my beautiful home.

Home

Make a Treasure Map showing the completion of your goals for your home. Look for pictures and phrases that capture both the physical surroundings and the qualities of the environment you are creating (e.g., brightness, openness, nurturing, calming, energetic, etc.).

Home

Make a list of personal affirmations for your home.

For example,

I feel joyful and relaxed in my beautiful home overlooking the ocean.
I am creating a place for love and laughter and friends in my gorgeous new condo.
I love creating fantastic, gourmet meals for my wonderful friends in my spacious, remodeled kitchen.

My positive affirmations about my home:

1.

2.

3.

4.

5.

Now spend ten minutes repeating them. Remember to focus on those wonderful qualities your home will embody as well as the physical details.

Close your eyes for a few minutes and visualize yourself having already reached your goals for your home. How does it look? How do you feel being in it? Hear your friends talking about it and complimenting you on it. Write about how that was for you:

Home

What I am grateful for regarding my home is:

1.
2.
3.
4.
5.
6.
7.
8.
9.
10.

etc.

My Successes

Make a list of things you feel you are or have been successful at in your life. Include things related to work, home, relationships, hobbies, school, sports–anything big or small–that has meaning for you.

For example,

1. *I am a good mother.*
2. *I am a great cook.*
3. *I learned how to play piano when I was six years old.*
4. *I successfully wrote a book.*
5. *I lost 30 pounds.*
6. *I am a great communicator.*
7. *I got excellent grades in school.*

Etc.

Things I have done successfully are:

1.

2.

3.

4.

5.

6.

7.

8.

9.

10.

Setting Yourself Up for Success

Take some time when you can relax and close your eyes. Now visualize a situation in your life where you've been afraid of failing. See yourself succeeding. See yourself happy and smiling and everything working out perfectly. Feel what it feels like to succeed. Hear the kinds of things people are saying to you–perhaps they are congratulating you on your success. Once you have completed the visualization, write about it below.

I am a great success at . . .

Write a paragraph or create a mind map of your ideal scene regarding success in your life.

For example,

My goals for creating success in my life for the next six months are:

1.

2.

3.

4.

5.

6.

7.

8.

9.

10.

etc.

Examples of positive affirmations that you can repeat regarding success:

Through my phenomenal success, I attract a wealth of emotional and financial support and opportunities for growth and service.

I am an excellent ________________, confidently creating demonstrated results that are appropriately recognized and rewarded.

I bring success, abundance and upliftment to all involved in my professional interactions.

I daily increase the value I create for myself, my family, and my organization.

I am finding increasing satisfaction and fulfillment in my day-to-day activities.

Make a Treasure Map showing the completion of your goals for creating success in your life. This can include things in every area–any accomplishment that you can make. For example, you could be receiving an award, winning a prize, having a terrific relationship, doing a great job at work, or being accepted in a degree program.

Success

Make a list of personal affirmations regarding success in your life.

For example,

I am so proud of my persistence and determination in creating success in every area of my life.

I love the feeling of success. I radiate confidence and success to everyone I meet.

My positive affirmations about success in my life:

1.

2.

3.

4.

5.

Now spend ten minutes repeating them. Keep focusing on how successful you already are.

Close your eyes for a few minutes and visualize yourself having already reached your goals regarding success in your life. How do you look? How do you feel? Hear yourself talking about your success. Write about your experience.

Success

What I am grateful for regarding success in my life is:

1.
2.
3.
4.
5.
6.
7.
8.
9.
10.

etc.

Listen to the tape, "Creating a Winning Attitude," from this packet. Write about what you learned, felt, or experienced from it.

Listen to the tape, "Nurturing the Inner Child", from this packet. Write about what you learned from your Inner Child.

Spiritual/Religious

Write a paragraph or create a mind map of your ideal scene regarding your own spirituality, religious or spiritual practices.

For example,

I am peaceful. I am spending time each day in meditation. I am dedicated to serving myself and others. I am tithing ten percent of my income to my church. I am sharing God's love with my family and friends.

Spiritual/Religious

My goals in the area of my spiritual or religious practices for the next six months are:

1.

2.

3.

4.

5.

6.

7.

8.

9.

10.

etc.

Examples of positive affirmations regarding spiritual/religious beliefs:

I am relaxed, joyfully trusting in God's plan that is unfolding perfectly for me.

With God's grace, and in harmony with His divine plan, I am attracting to me those who, with my God-given skills, I can serve and be served by for the highest benefit of all concerned.

Every day, I am looking through the eyes of loving.

I am spending at least 30 minutes each day in meditation.

I experience an ever-increasing awareness of God as I work, play, and sleep.

I am making loving the most important part of my behavior

(Feel free to adapt these to fit your personal beliefs)

Spiritual/Religious

Make a Treasure Map showing the completion of your goals for your spiritual or religious practices. You might want to include religious symbols or icons that are significant, phrases or sacred writings that have special meaning for you, or pictures of yourself in a harmonious, joyful, uplifted state. If you have pictures of your family and friends at religious or spiritual observances–such as holidays or special services or holiday meals–you can put those in, too. You could also use pictures of nature, things that express beauty, joy and love, or symbolize your spiritual or religious experience.

Make a list of personal affirmations for your spiritual or religious beliefs.

For example,
I am spending at least 30 minutes every day in meditation.
I am tithing ten percent of my income every month to my church.
I am attending my small group meeting every week.

My positive affirmations about my spiritual or religious beliefs and practices:

1.
2.
3.
4.
5.

Now spend ten minutes repeating them. Make this an uplifting, joyful experience. If you do any type of prayer, meditation, quiet time or spiritual exercises, this might be a good time to go into that.

Close your eyes for a few minutes and visualize yourself having already reached your goals for your spiritual or religious practices. How do you look? How do you feel? Write about your experience:

Spiritual/Religious

What I am grateful for regarding my spiritual or religious beliefs and practices is:

1.

2.

3.

4.

5.

6.

7.

8.

9.

10.

etc.

Write a paragraph or create a mind map of your ideal scene regarding our world.

For example,

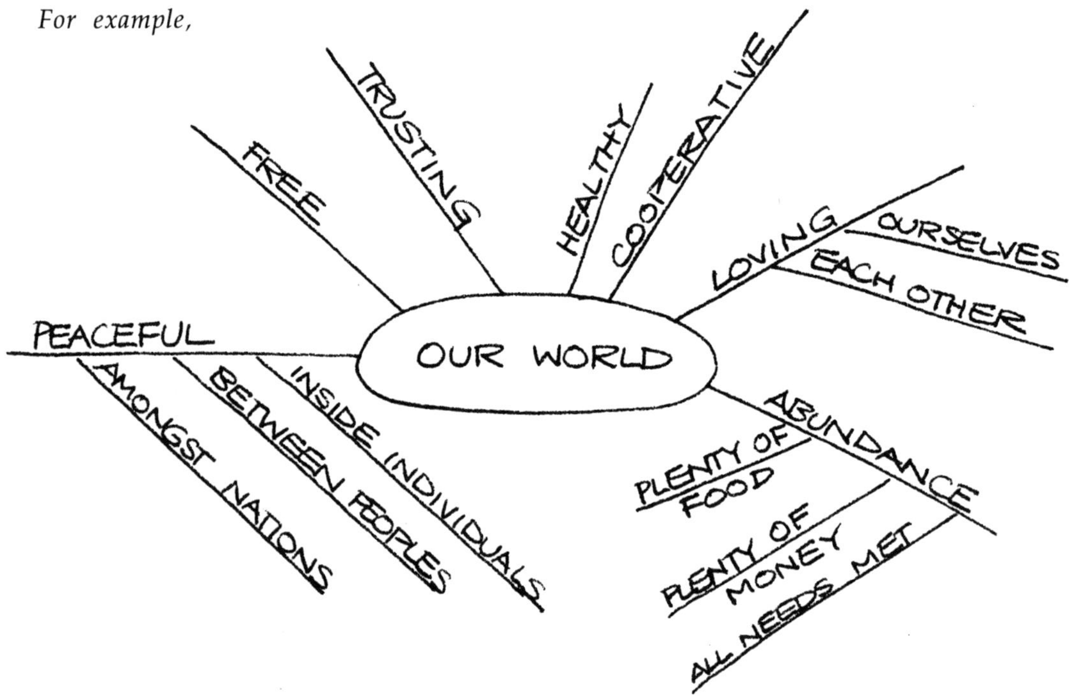

My goals for the next six months regarding how I can contribute toward making our world a better place are:

1.

2.

3.

4.

5.

6.

7.

8.

9.

10.

etc.

Examples of positive affirmations that you can repeat regarding our world:

I am confidently interacting with people as I am serving and expanding my loving.

I am creating a major impact, applying small things consistently and strategically.

I am risking, reaching out, and making a difference in our world.

Our world is consistently moving into greater balance, harmony, freedom, joy, and abundance.

I am creating and experiencing a major win for all involved with the community service projects.

Every day, peace and harmony is increasing in the hearts and minds of every person on the earth.

I am a positive influence in my community, inspiring my friends and neighbors to greater levels of cooperation, friendship and appreciation.

The World

Make a Treasure Map showing the completion of your goals regarding how you can contribute toward making the world a better place. Include things that really capture the qualities that you want to have more of in your world.

Make a list of personal affirmations for your vision of how wonderful the world could be.

For example,

I am doing everything I can to make our world a better place by sharing my love, joy, and abundance with everyone who comes my way.

My positive affirmations about the world:

1.

2.

3.

4.

5.

Now spend ten minutes repeating your affirmations. Keep holding your vision and sharing it with others.

Close your eyes for a few minutes and visualize yourself having already reached your goals regarding your contribution toward making our world a better place. How do you look? How do you feel? What does that sound like? Write about what that was like:

The World

What I am grateful for in our world today is:

1.

2.

3.

4.

5.

6.

7.

8.

9.

10.

etc.

Child Play

Look into the eyes of a baby. See the loving, the purity, the innocence. Make a list of the beautiful, positive things you see.

1.

2.

3.

4.

5.

6.

7.

8.

9.

10.

Now ask yourself, "If this baby is a mirror of me, what wisdom can I learn from looking in his/her eyes?" Write your answer on this page.

Play with a baby. Let your joy and your loving come out in the most easy and simple ways. If you want, you can write about this experience later. Be sure to reflect on how the beautiful things in the baby are the things that are beautiful about you.

Child Play

Play a game with children. As you enjoy them and give them encouragement, enjoy yourself and inwardly give yourself encouragement. Write about the experience you had letting your inner child come out to play.

Bake cookies with a child. While you are doing this, give the little child inside of you permission to come out and play. (Remember to keep the adult part of you present enough to act safely and responsibly.) Make this experience as fun and joyful as you can. Ask your young friend what their favorite kind of cookie is, what they would like to go with it (e.g., milk, ice cream, soft drinks, etc.) and if they would like to share their treats with anyone. Afterwards, you can write about the experience on this page.

Make a surprise treat for your family and friends. While you are preparing the treat, focus your loving on each person and think about why they are special to you. Acknowledge yourself for all the loving and caring you are expressing by doing this. Afterwards you can use this page to write down any thoughts or feelings you had.

Go out to an elegant brunch with friends. You might want to go to a special restaurant you like or maybe one you have always wanted to go to. Remember the special touches–buying flowers, asking the musicians to play someone's favorite song, complimenting your friends' appearance. Also, you might want to share your joy with the people serving you by asking their names and expressing appreciation for their work. Use the space below to record any special memories.

Nature

Go for a walk in nature. Enjoy the beauty of the things around you (e.g., trees, grass, flowers, birds, sky, animals, etc.).

If nature is a reflection of who you are, what would it be saying about you? (What's beautiful about you?)

Write at least one paragraph about how what you saw in nature is a reflection of yourself.

Spend time being with and looking at a tree. Ask it for its advice on how to live a happy life.

Write about or draw a picture of the tree's message and what you learned from it.

Spend time being with and looking at some flowers. Ask them for their advice on how to live a happy life.

Write about or draw a picture of the flowers' message and what you learned from it.

Spend time being with and looking at a rock. Ask it for its advice on how to live a happy life.

Write about or draw a picture of the rock's message and what you learned from it.

Spend time being with and looking at the daytime sky–the sun and the clouds. Ask it for its advice on how to live a happy life.

Write about or draw a picture of the sky's message and what you learned from it.

Spend time being with and looking at the night sky–the moon and the stars. Ask it for its advice on how to live a happy life.

Write about or draw a picture of the sky's message and what you learned from it.

Spend time being with and looking at some grass. Ask it for its advice on how to live a happy life.

Write about or draw a picture of the grass's message and what you learned from it.

Plant a garden or pot some plants. While you are doing this, be aware of your surroundings. Is the sun shining? Is there any breeze? Is it hot or cold? Feel the texture of the soil, the plants, the water. Experience the simple joy of what you are doing. Afterwards you can write about it on this page, or draw a picture or attach a photograph.

Go for a walk. Notice all the beauty around you, especially the things you don't usually notice. Do you see things differently? How could you look at the beauty inside yourself and see it differently, also?

Go for a walk. Smile at each person you meet. Don't worry about whether or not they smile back–just share your joy and loving.

Get a bunch of flowers. Go for a walk and give a flower to each person you meet and wish them a happy day. Note their reaction.

Go for a walk and pick up trash and clean up your neighborhood. Afterwards, reflect on what that was like. How does that make you feel?

Go for a walk. Smile and say hello to each person you see. What was that like?

Spend a day in total silence. Write about what you experienced throughout the day–how did you feel? What was it like? What new things did you learn?

Get comfortable and spend 20 to 30 minutes relaxing. Close your eyes. Use your creative imagination. In your mind, go to a quiet place in nature. Observe the sights, the sounds. Enjoy and breathe in the peacefulness. Afterwards, write or draw a picture about your experience.

Take 20 to 30 minutes to relax. Get comfortable–sitting in a chair or lying down. Close your eyes and visualize a fountain of pure white light above your head showering down around you and through you . . . a pure white light . . . filling you, surrounding you and protecting you. Breathe in that pure white light and allow it to fill your entire beingness, bringing with it a sense of peacefulness and calm.

Listen to a relaxation or meditation tape.

Read a book that is of an uplifting nature.

Give yourself a massage. Use your favorite body lotion or oil. Put loving into every part of your body.

Spend some quiet time in nature, at the beach, or in a park.

Take some time to listen to your favorite music. Close your eyes. Relax. Enjoy.

Fun

Make a list of the things you have wanted to do in the areas of fun, recreation and entertainment.

For example,

1. *Invite friends to our house for dinner.*
2. *Go to a movie.*
3. *Go for a hike.*
4. *Take a trip to Hawaii.*
5. *Go dancing.*

Do at least two things on your list in the next two weeks. Write about your experiences.

What hobby or sport have you been wanting to learn (e.g., skiing, jogging, playing the piano, etc.)?

What is your next step?

When will you take that action?

See a funny movie or show.

Read a joke book.

Go dancing with a friend.

Rent a convertible and ride with the wind around you.

Sing songs around the piano with friends.

Go out for a special dessert with a friend.

Happiness

Interview a few people over 60 and ask them what they have found to be their keys for living a happy life.

Keys for living a happy life:

1.

2.

3.

4.

5.

6.

7.

8.

9.

10.

Today, make loving a part of all of your communications. At the end of the day, write about your experience.

Today, look for all the good and positive things in everyone and everything you see.

Today, see how many people you can catch doing something good!

Today, see how many times you can catch yourself doing something good.

About Insight Seminars

Insight Seminars is the continuing education division of the University of Santa Monica, with headquarters in Santa Monica, California.

Insight offers educational seminars and workshops to thousands of individuals annually in over 25 major cities in the United States and in England, France, Germany, Australia, Sweden, and South America.

The seminars and workshops are designed to assist people in enhancing self-esteem, increasing personal efficiency, and developing individualized expressions of service as a source of inner satisfaction and as a means of making a positive impact on the world.

The Gift of Giving program provides individuals with the opportunity to participate in a six-day educational and motivational seminar and to contribute only that which is within their means as remuneration. Some of the major topics covered in the seminar include

- Enhancing self-esteem
- Overcoming guilt and resentment
- Giving and receiving feedback
- Improving relationships
- Building cooperation and dealing with competition
- Building strength vs. protecting weakness
- Taking responsibility and accepting accountability
- Creating success
- Overcoming fear and avoiding blame
- Building acceptance and avoiding judgment

Special teen seminars, children's programs, and self-esteem workshops including ACE (Achievement and Commitment to Excellence) are offered through Insight's Family and Youth Division, both in the public schools and for the general public. Through these specialized programs, our youth are given the opportunity to work in nurturing environments with gifted facilitators on themes and issues that assist them in developing greater social responsibility, more effective peer and adult communication, and greater self-esteem.

Corporate education programs presented by the Insight Consulting Group offer state-of-the-art programs to Fortune 500 companies, as well as small and mid-sized firms that desire tools and techniques for implementing high performance management, expanding productivity skills, increasing motivation, and reducing stress.

Free introductory information about any of the above programs may be obtained by contacting

INSIGHT SEMINARS
2101 Wilshire Boulevard
Santa Monica, CA 90403
(213) 829-9816
(800) 777-7750

BOOKS TO ENHANCE SELF-ESTEEM

YOU CAN'T AFFORD THE LUXURY OF
A NEGATIVE THOUGHT
John-Roger and Peter McWilliams.
Los Angeles, CA: Prelude Press, 1988.

WEALTH AND HIGHER CONSCIOUSNESS
John-Roger. Los Angeles, CA: Mandeville Press, 1988.

RELATIONSHIPS: THE ART OF MAKING LIFE WORK
John-Roger. Los Angeles, CA: Mandeville Press, 1986.

ONE MINUTE FOR MYSELF
Spencer Johnson, M.D. New York: Avon Books, 1985.

WHAT TO SAY WHEN YOU TALK TO YOURSELF
Shad Helmstetter. Scottsdale, AZ: Grindle Press, 1986.

RELEASE YOUR BRAKES
James Newman. New York: Warner, 1977.

TEACH ONLY LOVE
Gerald G. Jampolsky, M.D. New York: Bantam Books, 1983.

LOVE IS LETTING GO OF FEAR
Gerald G. Jampolsky, M.D. New York: Bantam Books, 1970.

TO GIVE IS TO RECEIVE
A Mini Course for Healing Relationships and Bringing About Peace of Mind
Gerald G. Jampolsky, M.D. Tiburon, CA: Mini Course, 1979.

THE PRECIOUS PRESENT
Spencer Johnson, M.D. New York: Doubleday & Company, 1981.

YOUR CHILD'S SELF-ESTEEM
Dorothy Corkille Briggs. New York: Dolphin Books, 1975.

WAY OF THE PEACEFUL WARRIOR
Dan Millman. Tiburon, CA: H.J. Kramer, Inc., 1984.

THE ROAD LESS TRAVELED
M. Scott Peck, M.D. New York: Simon and Shuster, 1978.

THE POWER OF POSITIVE STUDENTS
Dr. William Mitchell and Dr. Charles Paul Conn. New York: Bantam Books, 1986.

LOVE
Leo F. Buscaglia. New York: Ballantine Books, 1972.

LOVING EACH OTHER
Leo F. Buscaglia. New York: Holt, Rinehart and Winston, 1984.

LIVING, LOVING AND LEARNING
Leo F. Buscaglia. New York: Ballantine Books, 1982.

LOVE, MEDICINE AND MIRACLES
Bernie S. Siegel, M.D. New York: Harper & Row, 1986.

HOW CAN I HELP?
Ram Dass and Paul Gorman. New York: Alfred A. Knopf, 1987.

THE GIFT OF ACABAR
Og Mandino and Buddy Kaye. New York: Bantam Books, 1978.

ILLUSIONS
Richard Bach. New York: Dell Publishing Co., 1977.

JONATHAN LIVINGSTON SEAGULL
Richard Bach. New York: Avon Books, 1973.

FEEL ALIVE WITH LOVE. HAVE A HEART TALK
Cliff Durfee. San Diego: Live, Love, Laugh, 1979.

AUDIO CASSETTE TAPE PROGRAMS

INSIGHT, THE AWAKENING HEART
A booklet and two tapes including

- Reawakening Heart Seminar
- The Forgiveness Process
- A Return Trip to the Inner Sanctuary.

Insight Seminars. Santa Monica, CA: Insight Publishing ,1986.

MANAGING ACCELERATED PRODUCTIVITY
Six audio tapes and a study guide adapted from the Insight Consulting Group's successful two-day seminar. Areas covered include

- Managing Productivity
- Exploring Limitations
- Effecting Lasting Change
- The Rewards of Creative Planning
- Developing a Personal Management System

Insight Consulting Group. Santa Monica, CA: Insight Publishing ,1987.

MEDITATIONS FOR CENTERING IN THE HEART
A set of four meditation cassettes

- The Inner Calm
- The Body Relaxation Meditation
- The Breathing Meditation
- The Centering Process.

John-Roger. Los Angeles, CA: NOW Productions, 1988.

RELATIONSHIPS
A set of five cassette tapes including

- Nine Ways to Strengthen Your Relationships
- Five Ways to Deepen Your Relationships
- Keeping Relationships Wholly Holy
- Communication in a Safe Space
- Effective Communication.

John-Roger. Los Angeles, CA: NOW Productions, 1988.

MUSIC TAPES FOR RELAXATION

MIRACLES: MUSIC OF THE SPIRIT FOR HARP, STRINGS AND WINDS
Rob Whitesides-Woo. Venice, CA: 1985.

SACRED JOURNEY
NOW Productions. Los Angeles, CA: 1980.

THE HEALER'S TOUCH
Max Highstein. Los Angeles, CA: Inner Directions, 1986.

GOLDEN VOYAGE
Bearns and Dexter. Culver City, CA: Awakening Productions, 1978.

FRAGRANCES OF A DREAM
Daniel Kobialka and Andy Kulberg. Belmont, CA: Li-Sen Enterprises, Inc., 1983.

PATH OF JOY
Daniel Kobialka and Andy Kulberg. Belmont, CA: Li-Sen Enterprises, Inc., 1983.

FROM HEART TO CROWN
Rob Whitesides-Woo. Upland, CA: 1986.

FAIRY RING
Mike Rowland. Milwaukee, WI: 1982.

SOJOURN
Music of the Spirit for Piano and Orchestra.
Rob Whitesides-Woo and Scott Fitzgerald. Upland, CA: 1986.

AUDIO CASSETTE SEMINARS TO ENHANCE SELF-ESTEEM

The following titles are taped seminars by John-Roger, the founder of Insight Seminars. They have proven very effective in promoting greater self-esteem for thousands of people around the world.

WHAT IS THE BOTTOM LINE OF CONSIDERATION?
IS THERE A TRUE THANKSGIVING?
THE HEART CAN KNOW ANYTHING
DOES IT DO ANY GOOD TO CRINGE?
CONSTRUCTIVE CRUDICISM VS. POSITIVE AFFIRMATION
WHAT IS WORTHY ABOUT YOU?
GUESS WHAT I HEARD ABOUT YOU?
EXCU-U-USE ME: A PLAGARISM
ALL THE PERFECT REASONS
PERSONAL EFFECTIVENESS VS. TAKING YOUR SPACE
BACK TO THE DRAWING BOARD
PERFORMANCE IS THE BEST APOLOGY
MOVING FROM PROTECTION TO CORRECTION
IS THERE REALLY A LOVING WAY?
GIVING UNTIL IT HELPS
GREATER LOVE HAS NO MAN
ROLE AND GOAL AND TOLL EQUALS SUCCESS
ARE YOU IN ALIGNMENT?
HOW ARE YOU SELLING YOURSELF?
WHAT IS LOVING COMMUNION?
ENTHUSIASM: GOD'S ENERGY

All of the above tapes and tape sets are available through:

THE INSIGHT STORE
2101 Wilshire Boulevard
Santa Monica, CA 90403

INSIGHT CATALOG SALES
(213) 453-0071

Dear Reader,

Please accept this certificate as a gift from my heart to yours–as my way of supporting you in taking your next step in your personal development and enhancing your self-esteem.

In Loving,

Candy Semigran

Gift Certificate

This certificate entitles you to a $50 discount for the Insight I Seminar or the Insight Self-Esteem Workshop.

To find out how to register and the dates and location of the seminars nearest you, please contact:

Insight Seminars
International Headquarters
2101 Wilshire Boulevard
Santa Monica, CA 90403

or call toll-free:
(800) 777-7750.

One-Minute Self-Esteem: The Gift of Giving, the source from which this workbook is derived, is the chronicle of the author's progress, set-backs and triumphs with her own self-esteem. She shares the simple but profound concepts that became the foundation in her journey toward inner peace and self-loving. Each chapter presents key concepts, practical exercises and activities that you can use to move yourself toward a deeper sense of well-being and self-appreciation.

One-Minute Self-Esteem: The Gift of Giving is an excellent resource for all of us who find ourselves on the continuing and often challenging journey toward a greater sense of self-worth and loving. It is the perfect companion to the exercises and activities presented in this workbook and tape set. It is also a great book to share with family and friends.

This book is available from

THE INSIGHT STORE
2101 Wilshire Boulevard
Santa Monica, CA 90403

INSIGHT CATALOG SALES
(213) 453-0071

You may also order additional copies of this workbook and tape package.

Prices:		
	One-Minute Self-Esteem:	$11.95
	250 Ways to Enhance Your Self-Esteem:	$35.00

Please add $2.00 shipping and handling for each copy or set.
California residents include 6½% sales tax

Candace (Candy) Semigran is Chief Executive Officer of Insight Seminars, the Continuing Education Division of the University of Santa Monica. Insight Seminars is an international organization with headquarters located in Santa Monica, California.

Candy's expertise in the areas of self-esteem and personal effectiveness is the result of 20 years of study in the fields of education, relationships, and professional service training. Her work as a trainer, author, and educator is directed toward assisting people in gaining greater self-awareness and inner peace with the conviction that this will also have an influence on world peace. To that end, she has traveled extensively throughout the United States, South America, Australia, Europe, and the Soviet Union and has led seminars and workshops for thousands of people worldwide.

Candy has been instrumental in developing an array of educational and self-improvement programs including self-esteem workshops, relationship seminars, success and integrity workshops, and service seminars which, she says, "teach you how to love yourself more and be of service not only to yourself but also to your family, co-workers, and community at large."

No stranger to the personal development process, Candy complemented her Bachelor of Arts degree in education from California's La Verne University with over 500 hours of personal enhancement training between 1973 and 1987.

Candy has received the Who's Who in Professional and Executive Women 1987 Achievement Award and has twice received recognition from Who's Who in California. She is a native of Los Angeles and currently lives in Santa Monica, California, with her husband.